Drawing Horses and Foals

Drawing Horses and Foals by Don Bolognese

A HOW-TO-DRAW BOOK
FRANKLIN WATTS
NEW YORK | LONDON

to Stefano Cusumano
a great artist
and generous teacher

Library of Congress Cataloging in Publication Data

Bolognese, Don.
　　Drawing horses and foals.

　　(How to draw)
　　SUMMARY: Instructions for beginning sketches
and following through to the finished drawing.
　　1. Horses in art — Juvenile literature. 2. Drawing
— Instruction — Juvenile literature. [1. Horses in art.
2. Drawing — Instruction] I. Title. II. Series.
NC780.B58　　　　743'.69'725　　　　77-3688
ISBN 0-531-00379-5 (lib. bdg.)
ISBN 0-531-15200-6 (pbk.)
Second Paperback Edition 1990

Contents

Drawing Horses and Foals

Introduction

A horse is galloping, its mane and tail flowing gracefully.

A horse is rearing on its hind legs, its neck arched.

A horse is grazing quietly. Suddenly alerted, its head comes up and its eyes and ears turn toward you.

Have you ever wanted to draw such scenes? If so, you have had the same feelings as many artists before you. For thousands of years artists have been fascinated and inspired by the horse. Some have shown its speed, power, and strength. Many others have pictured the horse as being graceful, the animal of perfect proportions. Whatever their reasons, artists have constantly tried to capture in art the spirit and beauty of the horse. This book will help you to express your feelings about the horse through drawings.

Chapter I
The Beginning .

THE METHOD

This method of drawing is very simple. There are no tricks and there is nothing to memorize. But you must look very carefully at everything. Then, practice until your hand and pencil do what you tell them.

To do this, you work in two basic ways:
1. Quickly, which we call sketching.
2. Slowly, which we call drawing.

Of course, both ways are considered drawing, but keeping them separate will make this method clearer.

SKETCHING

A sketch is always done in a short time. It may take from a few seconds to ten or fifteen minutes to do. You sketch when you want to capture quick movements, or a particular action or mood. Sketching will train your eyes to be alert, and your hand to be quick.

Sketching is also useful in working out picture ideas. In a short time you can experiment with many different ways of designing a picture.

Sketches, then, are notes and preparations for future pictures. Pictures that will be either larger or more detailed than the sketches. This brings us to the second part of the method, the drawing.

DRAWING

A drawing takes longer than a sketch—no matter how small it is or how simple. A drawing requires a careful study of your subject. The better you know your subject, the more you can tell about it in your art. For example, the sketch of the hoof tells us its general shape, action, and position. The drawing, however, tells us much more. You can see the bone structure, the muscles, the texture of the hair, even the type of horse. Naturally, the drawing took more time, both in the observation and the doing. Sometimes a large, detailed drawing can take days to complete. But don't be discouraged. Drawing is not racing; speed does not matter. The more observation and practice you put into your drawing the better you will become. Date your sketches and drawings, and you will have clear proof of your progress.

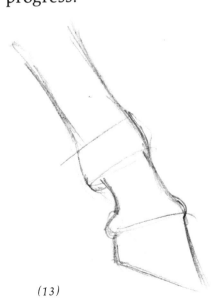 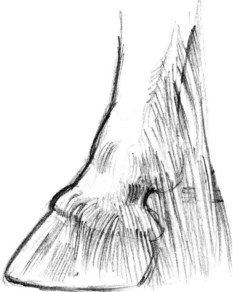

DRAWING AIDS

Photographs To help you in sketching horses in action, you can use photographs. Photograph and sketch a specific horse from many angles. Collect photos of horses trotting, cantering, jumping, or performing other actions.

Sculpture Sculptures of horses are also helpful. Many of our parks and museums have equestrian sculpture. These are particularly good models when you plan to spend a long time on a drawing. This was done by many famous painters of the past. They would do careful drawings of the great horse sculptures of their time. These "working drawings" or studies, as they were sometimes called, were then used as references for their paintings. These studies were so valuable that they were sometimes passed on to the next generation of artists.

The drawings and paintings of other artists can also be a source of help.

Toys Toy horses can also be used as models for drawing. They are especially helpful if you are planning a picture with many horses. Just set them on a table, and you have a miniature scene.

ART SUPPLIES

Small pocket pencil sharpener.
Sandpaper block—this gives an extra-fine point, especially with harder pencils.

Pencil—an ordinary no. 2 pencil is fine. If you wish a greater range of tones, use drawing pencils with leads of varying darkness. A good range would be from an H pencil (on the light side) through the Bs (HB, B, 2B, and 3B) up to a 4B pencil (soft and dark).

Eraser—Kneaded eraser—very good for erasing small areas or for lightening strokes. Just press the eraser on the line, don't rub, and the eraser lifts off some of the lead. Gum and plastic erasers—good for cleaning large areas. The plastic eraser does not scratch the paper.

Felt pens—the water-soluble ones with fine points. Brushing over the lines with a wet brush produces a tone.

Paper—any good bond paper, as long as it is neither too rough nor too thin.

Lightbox for tracing—the simplest lightbox is a window with light coming through. Tape a drawing to a window pane. Tape a fresh piece of paper over it and trace. A simple desk-top lightbox can be made by putting a piece of glass (frosted glass is better than clear glass) in a frame built up enough so that a light bulb can be placed underneath it.

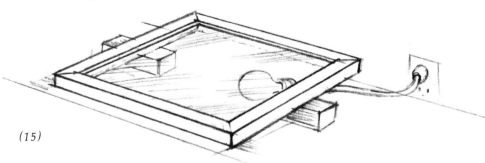

PARTS OF THE HORSE

Here are the words used to describe different parts of the horse. They will be used in the instructions to help you locate a particular place on the horse or to compare the same parts on different breeds. Refer back when necessary, and you will find they quickly become familiar.

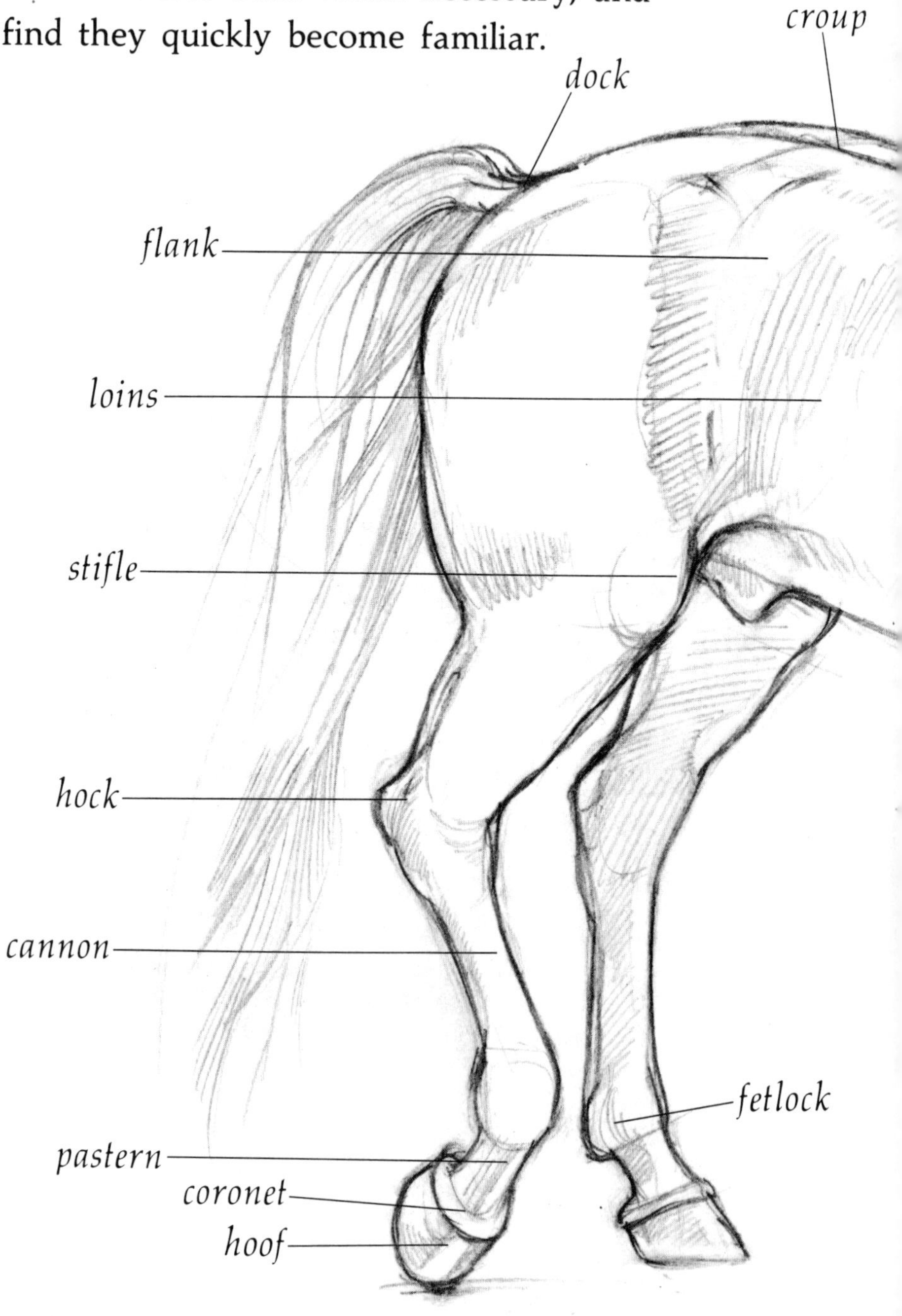

croup

dock

flank

loins

stifle

hock

cannon

fetlock

pastern

coronet

hoof

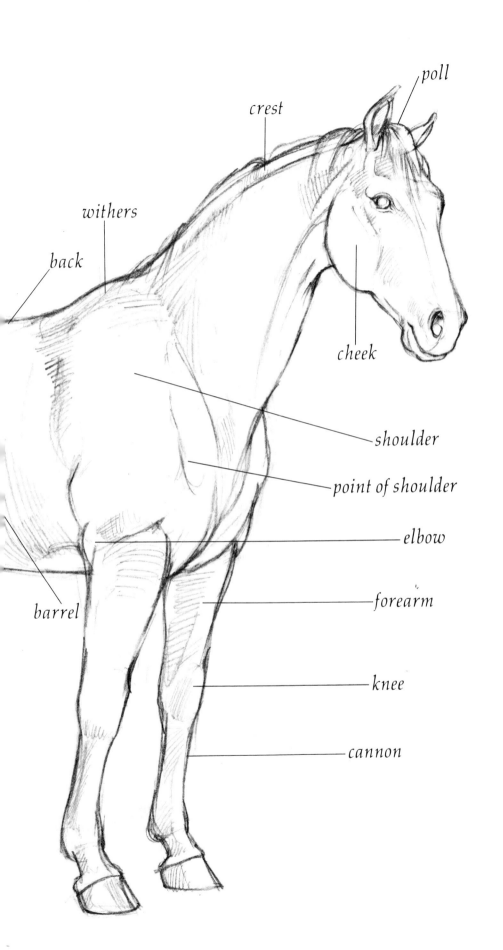

poll

crest

withers

back

cheek

shoulder

point of shoulder

elbow

forearm

barrel

knee

cannon

Chapter II
Drawing Step-by-Step

In this chapter you will see a drawing as it develops. From the very first step to the last step (the drawing facing this page) you will see what is being done and why.

You may ask questions: why the shadows are in one place and not another; or why certain lines are emphasized rather than others. The notes with each stage of the drawing are the answers and instructions.

The first step is the sketch. For an artist, sketching should be a daily activity. Carry a sketchpad and think of your eyes and hand as a camera. Your sketchbook will fill up quickly and will always be a source of ideas for your work.

THE SKETCH

In doing the sketches for this drawing, concentrate on situations with only one horse.

Sketch the horse in many different places and positions. Outside, in the barn, in motion, at rest. In all of these quick sketches, try to select the lines that best express the action.

The line from the tail along the back to the neck and head.

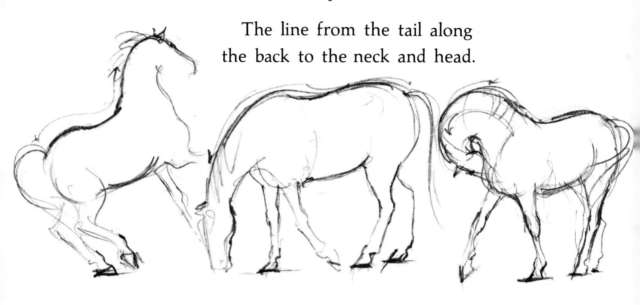

The position of the legs. Which legs are supporting the weight of the horse?
The direction of the head.
The flow of the mane and the tail.

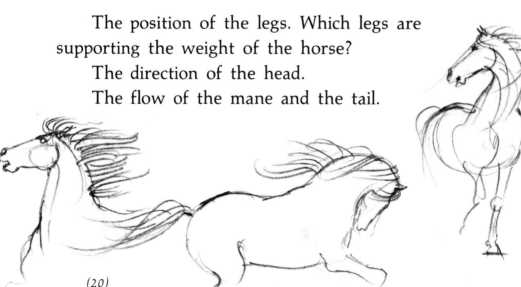

(20)

In these preliminary sketches also try to indicate light and dark. Shading or strokes that suggest shadows are helpful in several ways.

They help to convey a mood or feeling.

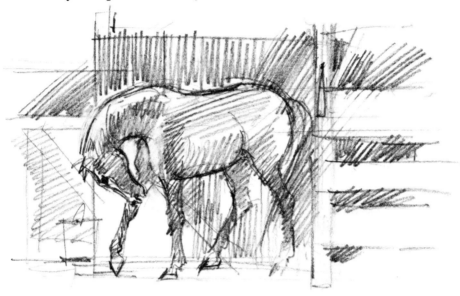

They give an indication of a particular place or setting.

They add form and substance.

After doing many sketches, look back through your sketchbook and select one.

This one was picked because it catches the excitement and eagerness of a horse ready to go out. They show in the tension of the neck as the horse turns in expectation.

(22)

THE TRACING

The next step is the tracing. A lightbox (see chapter 1) makes this very easy.

In tracing the original sketch, try to make the horse's action and position clearer. Begin to define the beams of the barn.

FORMS AND STRUCTURE

The next step is to strengthen the forms of the
horse. The structure of the horse is more clearly
drawn from the hoof up to the cheekbone.
The barn setting is also drawn
with more detail.

(24)

You have to show the weight on the horse's right leg. In the detail below see how firmly the hoof is hitting the ground. The stiffness of the leg shows the pressure. This creates a strong contrast to the uplifted leg. In both legs, however, the joints and bones are brought out and defined to show their hardness.

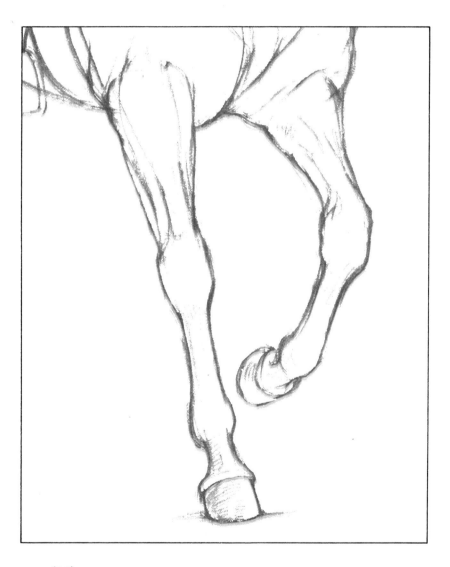

ROUNDNESS

The next stage of the drawing deals with the roundness of the forms. Work on the shoulders, hindquarters, and barrel. Use the shading to bring out the bulk and weight of the body. The strokes follow the direction of the curve of the body.

This close-up detail of the saddle illustrates how you can further emphasize roundness of form. All of the strokes on the barrel follow the saddle girth around the body. The saddle also helps to establish the perspective of the horse's body as it goes back in space. Notice the pencil strokes. They are wider apart at the front and closer as they go back on the body.

THE FINAL STAGE: TONES AND TEXTURE

The drawing below is the same as on page 18.
In this final stage tone and texture are added.
Add accents of tone to the
neck and head to give
a sense of drama.

The tones added to the tail and mane show movement. At this point more detail could be added to the horse and the barn; however, if you have achieved what you wanted, there is no need to add more.

The close-up of the head shows how the addition of tone to the eyes and neck helps to get the desired effect.

The darker tone brings out the tension in the neck. The darkness around the eyes contrasts with the splash of bright light on the front of the head. Together they help give a feeling of alertness and spirit.

Chapter III
A Horse: Piece by Piece

Now that you have produced a drawing in stages, you should do the same with the horse.

Focus on drawing different parts of the horse. Without studying a skeleton or memorizing the names of muscles or bones, you can see how a horse is put together.

THE HOOF:
a firm foundation

The hoof is graceful in its shape. However, it must be round and solid. Never draw one that is too small or too weak-looking for your horse.

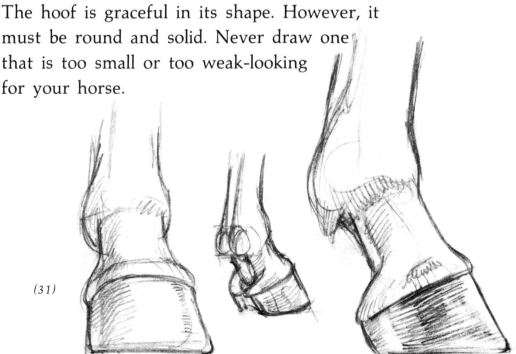

THE LEGS:

support, action, speed

In drawing the legs you must emphasize the joints—especially the hocks in the hind legs and the knees in the forelegs. This will help you avoid drawing rubbery legs. A tight bend in the leg gives a horse a spirited look and conveys a sense of energy and speed.

Notice how the muscles bunch up as the hind leg is brought up.

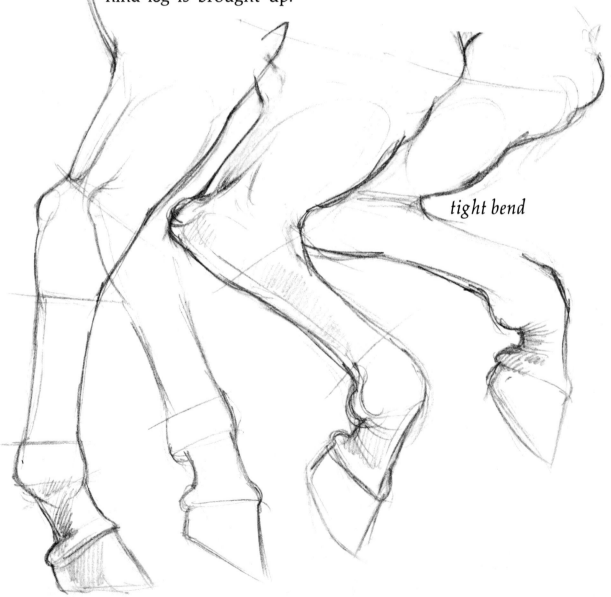

tight bend

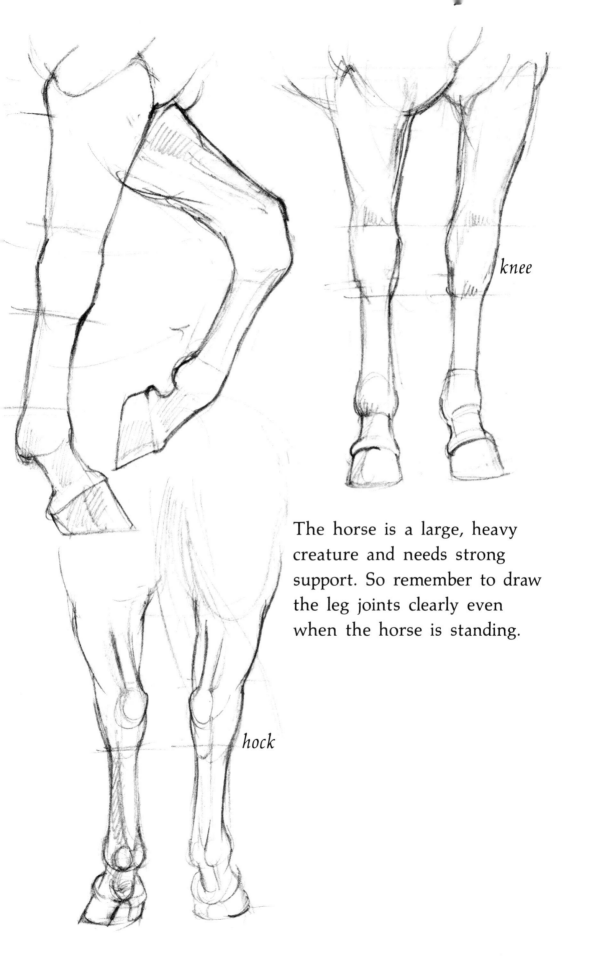

knee

hock

The horse is a large, heavy creature and needs strong support. So remember to draw the leg joints clearly even when the horse is standing.

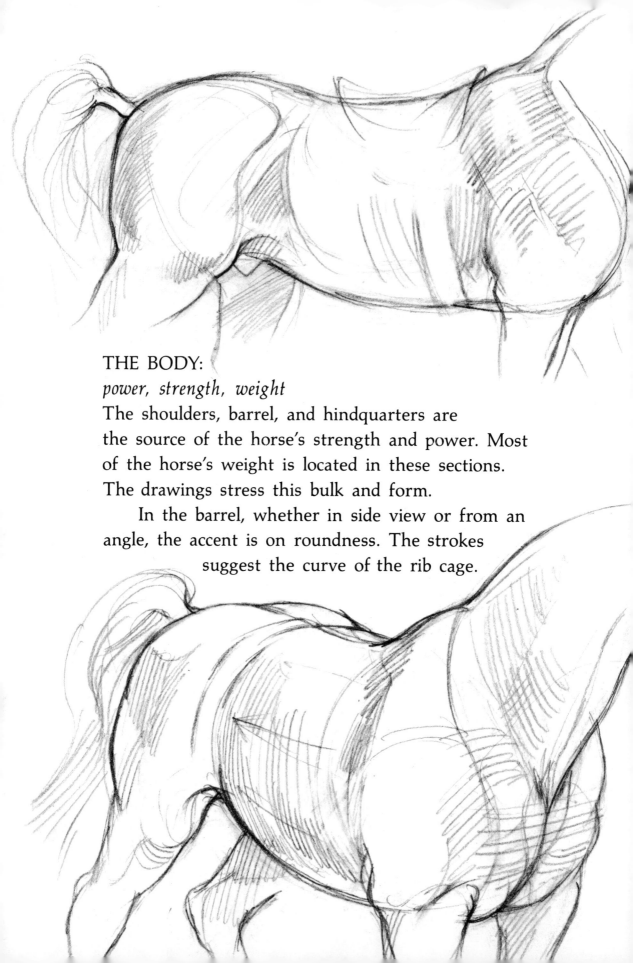

THE BODY:
power, strength, weight

The shoulders, barrel, and hindquarters are
the source of the horse's strength and power. Most
of the horse's weight is located in these sections.
The drawings stress this bulk and form.

In the barrel, whether in side view or from an
angle, the accent is on roundness. The strokes
suggest the curve of the rib cage.

When the horse rears, the pencil
strokes should be farther apart,
indicating the expansion
of the rib cage.

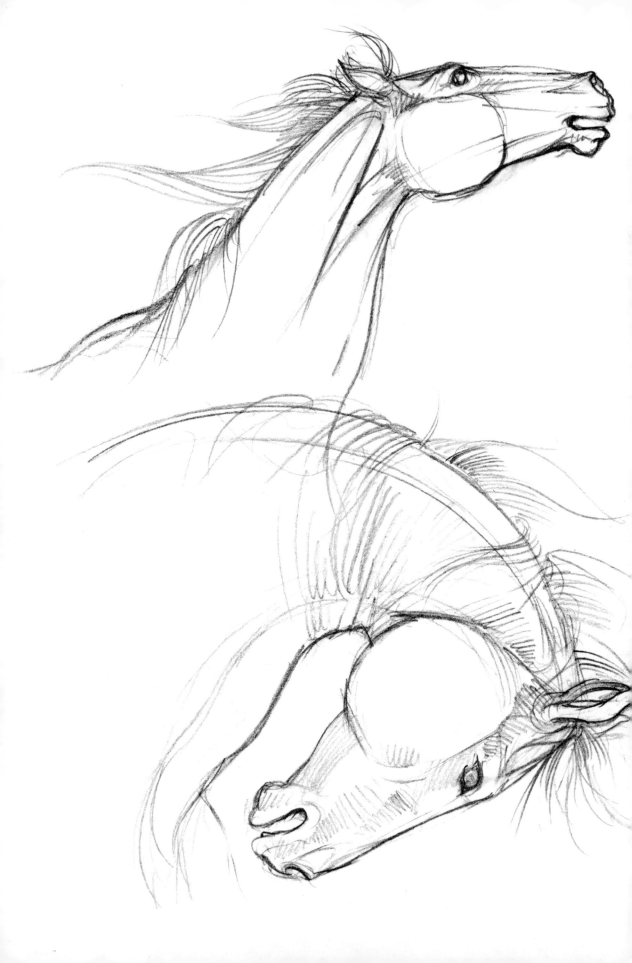

THE NECK:
grace, animation, tension

The neck is a very expressive part of the horse. The muscles stand out when the horse is straining in any one direction. Crowning the neck is the mane. The flow of the mane is an aid in giving a sense of movement to your drawing.

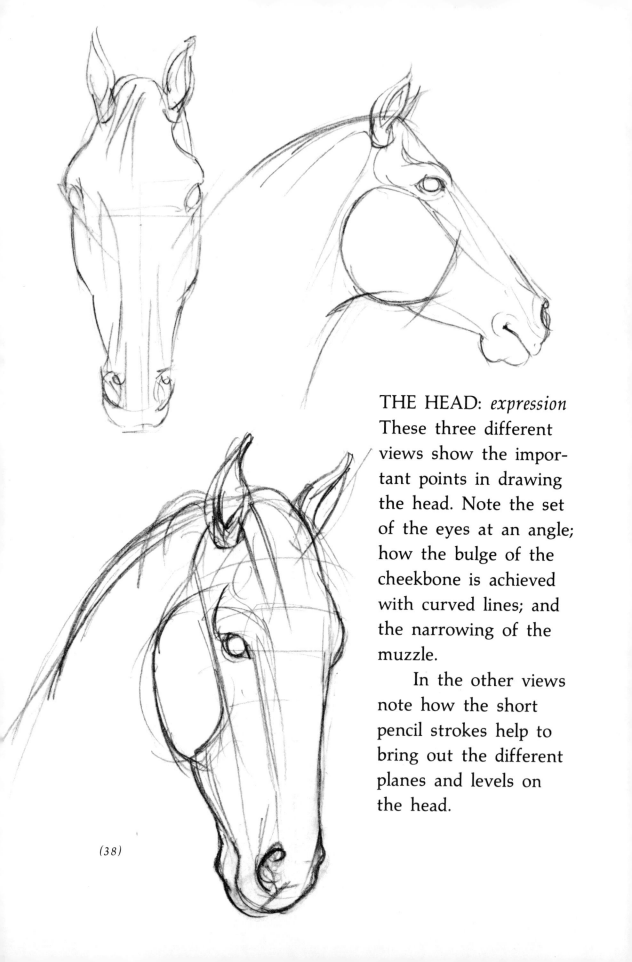

THE HEAD: *expression*
These three different views show the important points in drawing the head. Note the set of the eyes at an angle; how the bulge of the cheekbone is achieved with curved lines; and the narrowing of the muzzle.

In the other views note how the short pencil strokes help to bring out the different planes and levels on the head.

(38)

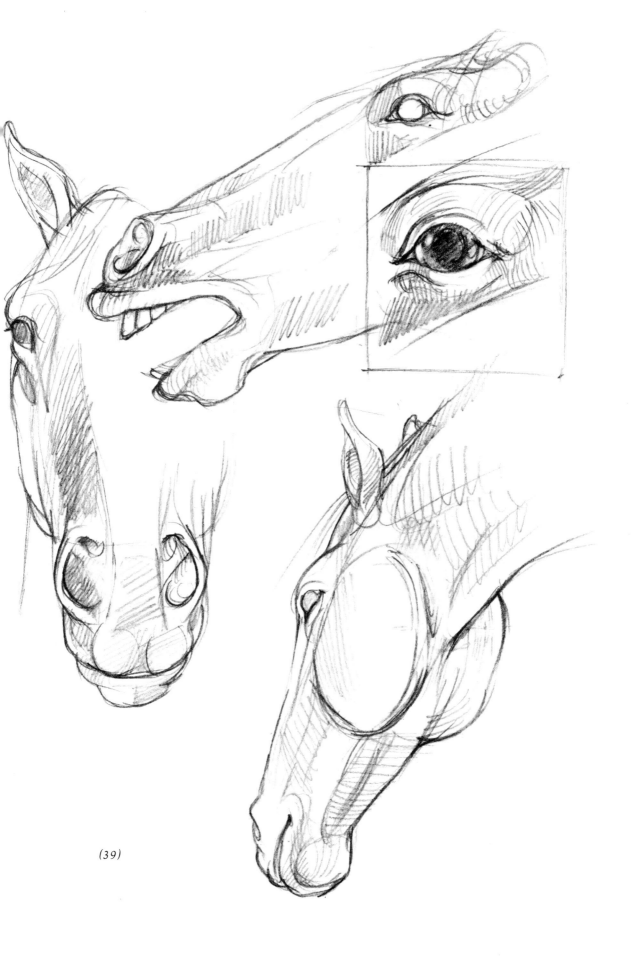

(39)

Chapter IV
The Young Horse

In drawing the young horse you must keep in mind the proportions. In general, a colt or filly is much "leggier" than a grown horse. The legs and joints in a young horse are much larger in comparison to the body than in a mature horse. The legs are knock-kneed, especially when very young. The ears and eyes are larger in relation to the rest of the head. The muzzle and hooves are smaller, and the tail and mane are shorter.

The foal in the drawing to the left is only a few days old. Note the size in relation to its mother.

note large knees

(42)

The leggy quality of the colt or filly is even easier to see when it is lying down or trying to get up.

In action drawings there is a sense of awkwardness. The young horse is not in full control of its body.

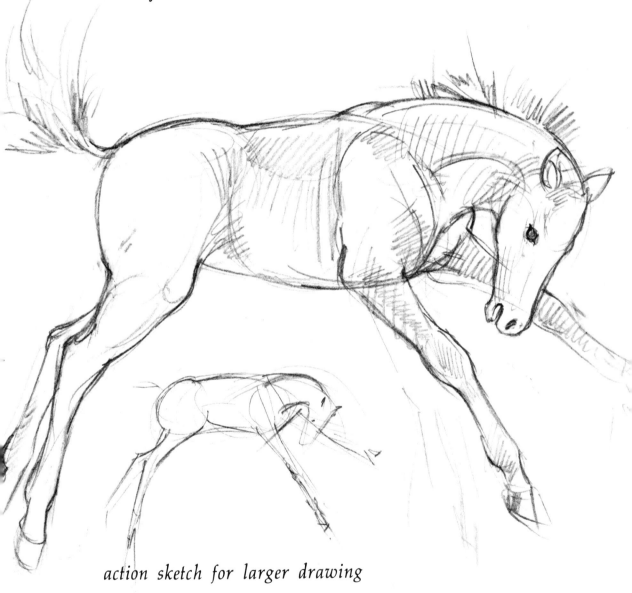

action sketch for larger drawing

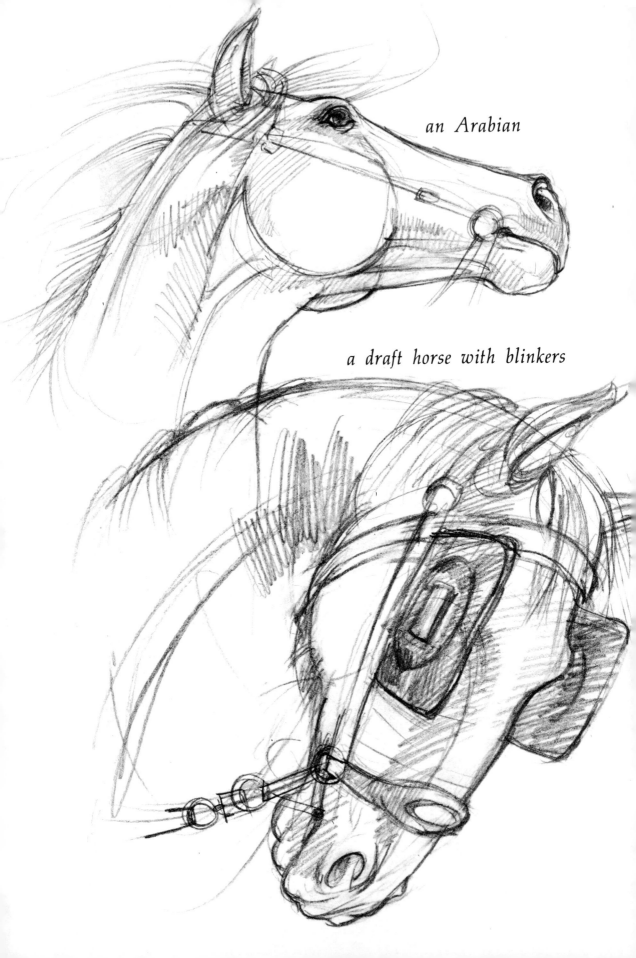

an Arabian

a draft horse with blinkers

Chapter V
A Horse for Every Occasion

All horses are not alike. These various types of horses are called breeds. Each breed of horse has a specific purpose and therefore a specific build and features.

There are horses bred for speed, such as racehorses. There are horses bred for strength called draft horses. There are even breeds that walk in a special way, or are particularly good at one gait rather than another. Some breeds are noted for their intelligence or for their gentle dispositions. Naturally not all of these characteristics are visible. Some of the more obvious physical differences between breeds are illustrated in this chapter. By understanding and emphasizing these distinctive features and differences, you will give your horse drawings individual character.

ARABIAN

The Arabian is considered to be the purest of all breeds. Many other breeds, the thoroughbred, for example, have Arabian blood in them.

The Arabian has several definite features that distinguish it from other horses.

Note the short back, and the very high arch of the tail and head. In action it has a high step.

(46)

The head is small in relation to its body. The eyes are set wide apart and slightly lower on the head than other breeds. They are also larger and more oval than in most horses. The skin around the eyes is dark. The muzzle is delicate with large, curved nostrils. The ears are small in proportion to the head.

Note the curve of the tail, back, and neck—leading to the head with its concave or dish-shaped profile.

THOROUGHBRED

The thoroughbred or racehorse is bred for speed. It is usually tall with long legs for long strides. The body is deep in the chest and narrow at the loins. The shoulders and hindquarters are well-developed, but not chunky as in draft horses.

The profile of the head is often more rounded and sloping than the Arabian. The nostrils are large as in the Arabian.

A racehorse is difficult to capture in an action sketch. If you use photographs as a guide, try to keep your drawings loose. Concentrate on the line of the back and neck and the positions of the legs. Note the position of the rider over the withers of the horse. This position gives the drawing a forward movement that suggests speed.

(49)

QUARTER HORSE

Compact, muscular, chunky—these are the words that describe a quarter horse. The short, muscular legs are suited for quick turns and short sprints.

In an action drawing, stress the round, chunky, muscles of the quarter horse in contrast to the longer muscles of the racehorse.

note roundness of muscles

MORGAN

The Morgan is an all-around horse. It is as compact and strong as the quarter horse, but more refined and graceful. The head, which is small, sometimes shows traits of the Arabian, with wide-set eyes and a slender, small muzzle. The neck is well-arched. The legs are sturdy but trim with well-shaped, small hooves.

The Morgan is a good
show horse both
with a rider and in
harness. Note the
high knee action and
the angle of the
hoof to the fetlock.

note angle

DRAFT HORSE

The barrel chest and bulging muscles show the power and strength of the draft horse. This particular breed of draft horse is a Clydesdale. Note its characteristic feathered hooves and its well-arched, wide, and muscular neck. The boy standing between the team gives an idea of the large size of a draft horse.

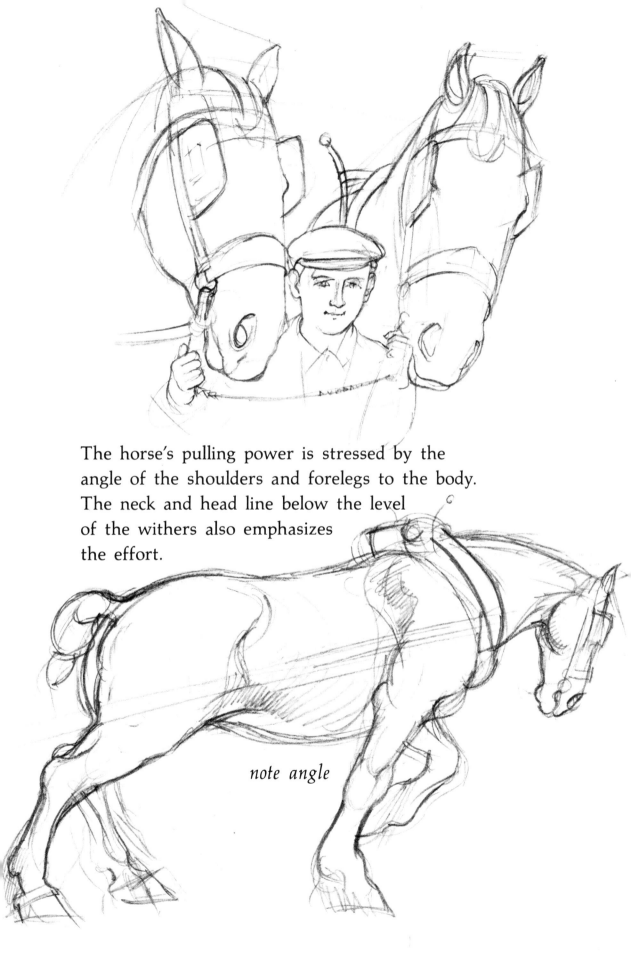

The horse's pulling power is stressed by the angle of the shoulders and forelegs to the body. The neck and head line below the level of the withers also emphasizes the effort.

note angle

THE PONY

All ponies are smaller than full-size horses. The Shetland pony is the smallest. They are usually no taller than thirty-eight or forty inches at the withers.

Notice the extremely short legs in proportion to the length of the body.

Other ponies such as the Hackney pony are usually better proportioned. High knee action is very characteristic of the breed. Note the size of the man in relation to the pony.

Shetland

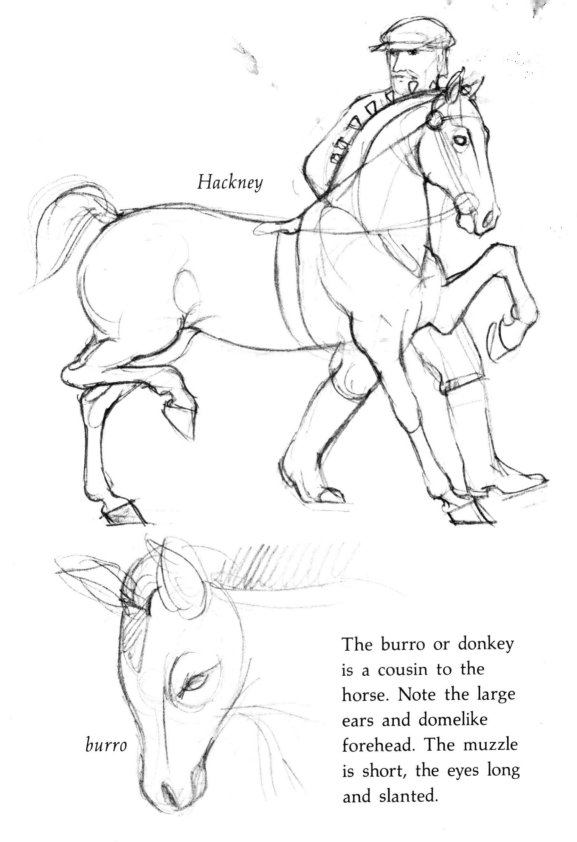

Hackney

burro

The burro or donkey is a cousin to the horse. Note the large ears and domelike forehead. The muzzle is short, the eyes long and slanted.

(57)

Chapter VI
Horse, Rider, and Cart

When you have more confidence about drawing
the horse, you may want to try something a bit
more difficult. Putting a rider on a horse or putting
a horse before a cart has its own challenge. There
are two points to remember.

The first is proportion. Whether you are
including a human figure or a cart or wagon with
your horse, you must be sure the sizes look
natural. There is no need to measure. Your eye
will tell you if one part of your drawing is out of
proportion with another.

The second point is the rhythm or
motion of horse and rider.

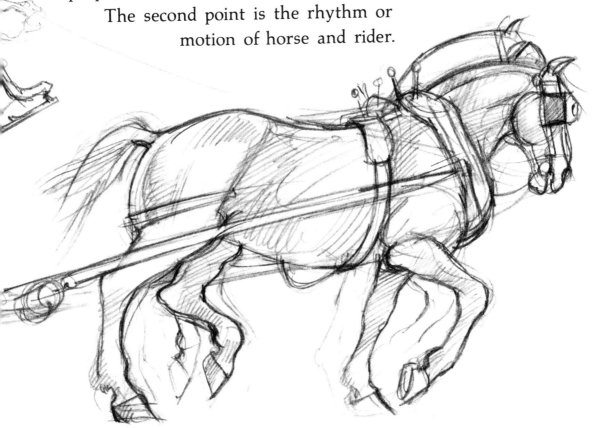

PROPORTIONS AND RHYTHM

To get some idea of proportions, look at the drawing below. Of course the relationship of the humans to the horse will change with the size of each.

The pictures on the right illustrate two contrasting points about the rhythm and motion of horse and rider.

The rider will either blend with the horse's action or be in opposition to it. The curves in the jockey's body blend with the curves of the horse. On the contrary the angle of the bronco rider to the horse shows the lack of unity.

HORSE AND RIDER

These four pages illustrate in part the action of mounting the horse and riding at three gaits: trot, canter, and gallop. In all the drawings note the rider's weight or pressure in relation to the horse.

Note how the weight of the rider is supported by the right hand while the right leg swings over the horse's back.

The most important point is to seat the rider in the right relation to the horse. In the small sketches note two common errors.

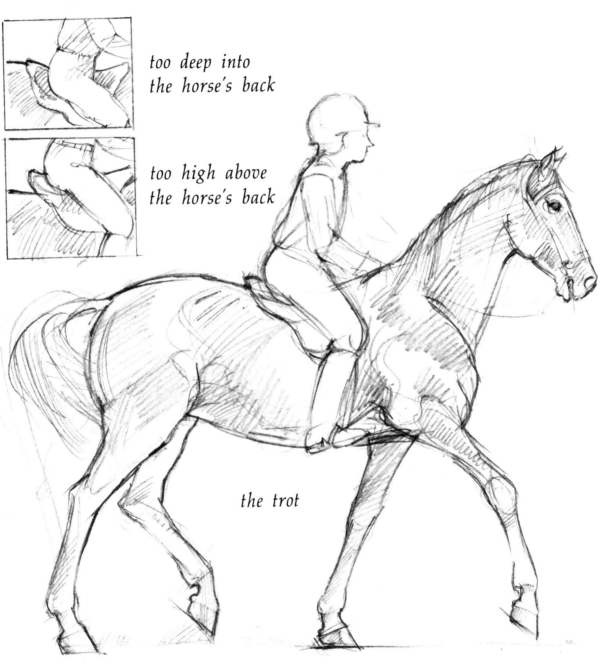

too deep into the horse's back

too high above the horse's back

the trot

CANTER AND GALLOP

The first beat of the canter. The rein forces the horse's head to the left. The left hind hoof is the only leg firmly on the ground.

In the second beat the left front and right hind feet hit the ground.

This is the
suspension stage
of the canter.
All four feet are
off the ground.

The suspension stage
of the gallop—note the
position of the rider.

HORSE AND CART

Proportion and correct placement are the most important points in drawing a horse and cart.

In the two small sketches note that what is nearest is largest. The guide lines left in the drawings show how the relationship between horse and driver is maintained in three views.

Note that the sketchy quality of the pencil strokes reinforces the sense of movement.

(67)

A Final Word

This book will be a valuable reference for you. Carry it with you when you go out sketching from life. Refer to it often as you attempt to understand the basic form and movement of the horse. As you progress in your ability to draw the horse, you will want to do more ambitious pictures. Try drawing in pen and ink, wash watercolor painting, or in oils and acrylics. When you reach this stage, remember that there are many fine and instructive examples of horse paintings. The list of artists (below) is only a short one, but it contains some of the best horse painters.

Rosa Bonheur
Edgar Degas
Frederick Remington
George Stubbs
Lucy Kemp Welch

About the Author

Don Bolognese is both the author and artist of a dozen books for young readers and has illustrated over 150 books for children and adults. He is a well-known painter, graphic designer, and calligrapher.

A graduate of the Cooper Union Art School, Mr. Bolognese developed and taught a comprehensive course on the art of the book at Cooper Union, Pratt Institute, and New York University. He has won awards from the American Institute of Graphic Arts, the Bologna Bookfair, the Society of Illustrators and many others.

He and his wife, author/artist Elaine Raphael, make their home in Landgrove, Vermont.